SMALL TALK

John Yamrus

Concrete Mist Press
York, PA 17403
USA
Temple1130@aol.com

Copyright © 2021 by John Yamrus

First Edition

Cover photo: Ashley Cox

Edited by Heath Brougher and Mish

Cover design: Concrete Mist Press and Mish

ISBN:

Manufactured in the United States of America

for
Kathy

Table of Contents

Introduction

By Michael Zielinski

John Yamrus has been a sublimely gifted writer for five decades, but his work never gets old. His words retain their swift gait without the aid of a cane, crutch or walker.

Indeed, it has been a prolific half century with two novels, over two dozen volumes of highly acclaimed poetry, two memoirs and a children's book.

I got to know John and his work when he was pitching his two memoirs and children's book on my television talk show. Needless to say, he is as glib as a conversationalist as he is a writer and our three chats were quite engaging and entertaining.

MEMORY LANE is a brief memoir of what it was like growing up in a Pennsylvania coal mining community in the 1950's. His second memoir *RMA* is another lyrical riff on his childhood with a title plucked from the pages of his high school yearbooks. You can sum up both memoirs with one word: magnificent. And I write that word without my pen dipped in hyperbole.

PHOEBE AND ITO ARE DOGS is a charming children's book of self-discovery based on the real-life experiences of brother-and-sister cocker spaniels that he and his wife Kathy raised from pups. I loved it despite being so old I cannot remember when I was a kid. Just a hunch but I think it was sometime before the invention of the transistor radio.

John disdains capital letters because he is a lower-case kind of guy…which makes him so damn likeable as a person and a writer.

He is a true artist who loves to read Proust and Kerouac while listening to the jazz of Miles and Monk. When it comes to writers and musicians, he only reaches for the top shelf.

His work has been described by acclaimed poet Milner Place as "…a blade made from honest steel, with the sharpest of edges."

That certainly slices to the heart of it.

John's writing, whether it be poetry, memoirs, novels, or a children's book, is a sumptuous smorgasbord of profound simplicity (no easy feat), wit, humor, talent that shouts to be read, insight, intelligence, introspection, individualism and inspiration. His work is crisp, descriptive and evocative.

In short, it is singularly John Yamrus.

At the considerable risk of facing summary execution for confessing this in a book of poetry, I am no fan of poetry -- having tripped all over iambic pentameter in high school English. But I am a big fan of John Yamrus's poetry. If this book is your introduction to his poems, I promise that you will be enchanted and mesmerized by *SMALL TALK*.

The book is bookended with poems touching on aging that resonated with me because, like John, I am a baby boomer.

John, of course, knows his work much better than I. In describing *SMALL TALK* to me before I read it, he wrote: "these poems (for the most part) don't tell the reader what to think about these people and these situations. they require input and involvement from the reader. even though they're short, i like to think they're open, active and alive."

After reading the book, his own words proved prophetic to me as surely as they will for you.

My personal six-pack of *SMALL TALK* favorites: "after," "puke-green," "his face," "Tony The Lip," "he" and "reluctantly". And narrowing it down to a mere six was harder than squeezing a cranky camel through the eye of a nano 4 mm 32-gauge needle, which is about as thin as two strands of hair.

Michael Zielinski is a playwright, screenwriter, novelist and columnist.

approaching 70:

at
this
point in the game,

i guess
i'm supposed to
be writing things like:

"sands at 70";
"the end is near";
and; "ode to my lost
and misspent youth"...

but,
i get the feeling
that i ain't done yet.

not by a long shot.

so,
give me
what you got.

i'm tough.

i
can
take it.

go
ahead.

i double-dog dare you.

i think

i was
28 at the time
and was in California
to do some readings and promote
this really bad novel i had just published.

and
they put me up
at a place called Sally's Motel

somewhere
out in Long Beach.

Sally's
had this little
u-shaped courtyard
that surrounded the pool

which
was empty
except for the cracks
and the weeds and the dirt

and
the shame.

and
my room
had two grimy beds
and a tv with a coat hanger antenna.

Sally's
was on its
last legs back then,

and
i'm sure
Sally was, too.

there actually *was* a Sally,

and
she looked
just like you would have pictured her,

with
the bleached blonde hair

and
the cigarette
jammed between her bright red lips.

and
the lobby
looked like every other lobby

in every
other sad motel.

it was
just this little hole of a room.

and
just behind the room
you could see where Sally lived.

and
the tv was on
and the whole place
smelled of whiskey, smoke,

and some
poor old dope's
broken, shattered dreams.

my life

didn't flash
in front of me,
or anything like that...

i
just
stood there,
on the corner,
thinking of Andy Warhol's glasses

and
humming
Hello Mary Lou, Goodbye Heart.

simple, huh?

and
here you are,
trying to get me to explain...

why?

it is
what
it
is.

you
either
get
it

or you don't.

or,
maybe
your tail's

just
waggin'

the
wrong dog.

after

the
rain,

reading Kerouac,

listening
to Cole Porter
playing quiet in the room,

there's
even birds
singing outside the window.

the
only thing
missing here

is
you.

puke-green

was
his favorite color.

it
was also
his favorite word

(or,
words, if
you wanted to
get technical about it).

anyway,
it was kinda sorta fitting
that he had already turned his
favorite color that Sunday morning

when
they found him

face down
under the Penn Street Bridge.

i sat in the sun room

reading
old books...
juvenile books, mostly.
stuff from back when i was a kid.

the
latest was
National Velvet,

the one
that got made into
a movie with Mickey Rooney
and a very young Elizabeth Taylor

back in 1944.

i remember seeing National Velvet
when i was in grade school.

it wasn't 1944.

it was
probably
the late '50s

and
my mother
used to let me
stay home sick all the time from school.

there was
even a year

when i came
this close to getting held back

because
i racked up
so many sick days,

but
they couldn't
keep me back because
i was quiet and had good grades,

and
anyway,
like i said,
i used to stay
home from school

while
my father
drove a delivery truck,

and
my mother
worked in one of
the many dress factories
that crowded the neighborhood.

my
grandparents
lived right across the street,

and
my grandmother

used to come and check on me at lunch,

bringing
jars of canned cherries

from
the tree they had,

and
i would sleep on the couch

watching
movies on tv,

and
i remember
National Velvet being one.

but,
i didn't
like it very much,
because there wasn't any

shooting in it,

and
it was
just for kids.

but,
it was
the only thing on,

so, i watched it.

the book
(and the movie)
is about a girl who's skinny and frail

and
a horse
that's big and tough

and
the girl wants
to run it in a race,
only the race isn't open to girls.

reading it now,
it's a pretty good book

and it
takes me back
to those days in 1959
when i got to stay home from school

and
lay on the couch
eating a great big bowl of cherries.

and
i had a pillow

and
a blanket

and
the room

and
the world
around me was

warm

and safe

and
good.

Ricky Lee

was
fast...

so fast,
he sometimes
didn't even leave

a
shadow.

not
that it
mattered much,

because
the things
Ricky Lee could

run from

were
never on his tail.
they were waiting for him...

right there...

patient.

at
the end
of Ricky Lee's

race.

he was

drunk
and more
than a little bit crazy

and
made the mistake
of leaving the live video feed

on
his computer open

and when
he was done reading his poems

all that
was left was this sad

drunk
old man
and the sound
of him walking from room to room

trying
to see where
the magic had gone.

looking

at
herself
in the mirror,

she
knew
she was
a promise
she couldn't keep.

one of my first publishers

is
retired
and living in France.

he's on
his second wife
and lives on a farm in the country.

every
now and then
he sends me these long, long e-mails

talking
about the wine,
the food, the people
and how much he loves his life

since he
ditched the first wife,
gave up writing, and moved away.

in
relative terms
he's on the near side of rich...

and,
i swear to god,
he got none of that

from
publishing me.

i
didn't even

answer his last two
e-mails.

i
didn't
know what to say,

other
than i hope
he's happy over there,

in
France,

with
his 2nd wife
and his fields and

his
wine.

when
you get
right down to it,

at the end of it all,

we both won...

he's
got France,

and
i've got

me.

his face

was odd.

tiny eyes that
squinted.

a forehead
so high

it made you
think
of

cathedrals

and

lips
that promised

laughter,
love,
or

fury.

they

both
knew it

do
any
one thing

long
enough

and
you'll
see things
to break your heart

if

you
are
the
first
of us

to
die,

how
will
i
ever
laugh

again?

Tony The Lip

was
older than he looked,

was
impressed
by the smell of his own farts,

lied
about everything,

never
held a job for long,

ate
everything,

drank
anything,

and
changed his shorts

no
more
than once a week.

Tony had
3 bad marriages,

4 shack-ups,

and
that one month he

never
cared to talk about.

i
always
liked Tony.

even

before
the hour sounds,

we
are already

sitting
with the dead.

we

are
less
than
ghosts.

the thing

about
you and me

(she said)

the
thing that
draws us together

is
we're
both fucked

and
we know it.

there's
no way out,

so
we
might
as well
enjoy the ride.

she
said it,

put down her glass,

turned

and
walked

26

out the door.

damn,
from that angle,

she
sure did
look good.

my friend Stanley hated the sun

he
hated
the heat.

ten years ago
his wife killed herself.

she
was in a car.

i don't know
how she did it.

it doesn't matter.

my friend Stanley was
big and fat.

he
kept every
room in his house
at 60 degrees.

my friend Stanley
loved
dogs,
bad jokes

and
beer.

my friend Stanley
is dead.

he

always
said

he
wanted

nothing

and
that's
exactly

what
he

got

my friend Bill

played guitar.

this was back in '72.

or,
maybe '73.

or,
maybe
before that,
because i don't really
remember and it doesn't really matter.

my
friend Bill
was maybe 23,
with long straight hair.

he
was skinny
and had spent time in Vietnam.

when
i first met him
he just got back from New York.

he
thought
he was a folk singer,
but, wasn't very good and
all he played were Dylan songs

and
when he laughed,

he
cackled.

Bill
would sit
in my kitchen
playing his beat up
old guitar and every now
and then he'd go out in his car

and
smoke
a joint because
my mother was in the
house and he didn't want her to know.

Bill sang thru his nose and
slammed the guitar so
hard he was always
breaking strings.

he was a good guy.

i knew him for
a year or two and then

we
lost touch.

somebody said
he

spent time
in the psych ward

at
the VA hospital,

and
when he got out
he went straight to his car,

drove
out to the woods

and
hung himself.

Bill never
made it
big.

they found his guitar
propped against
the tree...

damn,
if it didn't
have a broken string.

she said

touch
spit to me

and
i sizzle.

that's
way too hot

he
said.

damn it,
pass the tequila.

reluctantly,

he
had to accept

the
fact that

he
was destined

to
become

a
criminal

and
go to jail,

or
grow the fuck up.

there
was no middle ground.

either
way, it was

a
permanent
lack of freedom.

i'm

right now
sitting out back,
listening to Chet Baker –
the James Dean of '50s jazz –
and reading me some Kerouac,

(*Big Sur*),

while
the sun
goes down
behind the fence
right in front of me.

how
god damn perfect

is
that?

she said

you
think
that silly,
stupid grin
makes you bulletproof,

don't you?

then,
just to be

a
bitch,
she went
and proved him

wrong.

i

made
the mistake

of
complimenting him

on
his poetry.

on
the strength

of
one poem,
he wanted me
to introduce him to

my
publisher.

when
i refused,
when i said
i'm sorry, but
i just don't do that,
he went crazy on me.

instantly,

i
went from

hit
to shit.

more
than anything
he so desperately

wanted
his fifteen minutes

of
fame.

well...
here you go, buddy...

here
you go.

**there was this woman in there and she
was big, and**

i can still see her,
with this way she had
of kinda walking on her toes,
with her head tilted to the side,

she
was all legs,
and like i said,
she walked on her toes.

that's
the part
i'll never forget.

she'd
go into the bar
and come back with
sandwiches, cigarettes,
candy and a Jack on the rocks.

i
was
just sitting there,
not asking for trouble...

just
staring at
her and them legs,
when she put down the Jack,
lit up a smoke, and punched me

in
the side

39

of the head.

then
she walked out
and never came back.

she
was 40 pounds overweight,

walked
on her toes,

and
was the best
god damn thing

i
ever
did see.

whisper

to
me,

she
said,

you
sound
like god.

sure,

lay
back,

relax,

have
some wine.

you

are
a single

blue
thought

mingling
with
my

black

after the reading

i
took
some of the money i made

and
stopped off at K Mart...

i
bought
a bag of dog food,

some
new underwear

and
a pack of gum.

i
didn't
need the underwear,
and no one complained too much

about
my breath,

so, maybe i didn't need the gum, either.

the dog food's another story.

truth
be told,
i just wanted
to be able to spend

some
of the money

i
made.

i
wanted
to feel that
all that standing around,

reading
my poems
in front of a crowd,

and
acting like a fool

was
somehow worth it.

it
didn't matter.

at
the end of the day,

they
had my books

and
i had
what little was left of my soul.

just
another

payday drunk,

hoping
to make it home

before
the light turned red.

he

was
a person
of promise,

living
among
other

persons
of promise.

one day,
the promise

ended,

and that
was the end

of
that.

i've been shit on...

this time
by a
bird
whose aim
was more direct,
on target
and effective
than any of
the critics,
who
dislike me,
my poems,
my attitude,
my way of writing
or
just
my way of
seeing things.

in
fact,
this bird
should write
a book
and call it:

*"John Yamrus is in my sights...lean,
mean and as i see him"*...

it's
a little long
for the title of a book,

but,

then,
that was

one
hell of a bird.

i'd
tip my cap
to him,

but,
like i said...

he's
got me
in his sights.

all

it
takes

is
time

and
time

will take

it
all

Nelly Big Bang

loved poetry.

loved
Charley Parker.

loved
funny hats,

old
mirrors

and dogs.

Nelly Big Bang

loved
standing in
the sun as it shone

through
the window,
shining, bright
and gold on the floor
of the asylum where he died.

one of

his
biggest regrets

was
that he was
too old to die young.

James Dean...
Janis...
Jim Morrison...
Hendrix...

they
all knew

exactly
what it took
to make the legend work.

and him?

what
did he have?

the apartment,
Marsha
and that damn old dog
with those three good legs.

if he
could just
figure out a way,

he'd

give it all up...

in
a heartbeat...

everything...

the
apartment,

Marsha...

even
that damn old dog.

maybe then,

if he
managed
to do it right,

dying young

would be

all
the immortality
he would ever need.

the

tiredness,

the
loneliness

and
the disappointment

hurt,

but,
what hurt
even worse,

was
that look

in
her eyes.

the
one that said

you
don't even matter.

Rick

was
this old
friend of mine
who gave me my first
and only award for poetry.

it was
near 3 in the morning

and we
were drunk
on cheap vodka,

complaining
how we couldn't
get published anywhere

and never
won any awards for our work

and
we were
standing on this corner

ready
to call it a night

and
he looked up
at the street sign
and saw that it was Wakefield Street

and
he handed me
the bottle and said:

*i now award you
the prestigious Wakefield Prize*

except
he was drunk
and couldn't say it very clear.

but,
like they
say in the books,
it's the thought that counts,

and that
was the first
and only award

i ever got

and Rick
went on to give up writing

and
playing the
piano and guitar.

and
he taught Econ
in a very well-known college

until

one day
he'd had enough

and
stuck his head

in
the oven,
looking, i suppose,
for whatever remained
of his music, his hopes, and his dreams.

"think of this

as just
another part of your job,"

she said,

as she
arranged
the lights around me...

and
my shirt...

she
took great care
to make sure the shirt

was
looking just right.

she said:
"if we don't
make you look good,
we don't get the posters up,

and
if we don't
get the posters up,

nobody shows,

and
the whole thing's
a great big waste of time.

this is
just another
part of your job."

right
then and there
i absolutely hated my job.

i
wished to hell
i was back there,

in my room,
with the shades pulled

and
the tv on.

this job
was something i never wanted.

the
only job
i ever really

needed...

was
this room,

these
poems,

and
you.

how

were
we
to know

we
were
happy?

most days

he
just sat
with the sun
coming in over his shoulder,

like something out of
a Robert Mitchum
movie.

he'd read
The Grapes Of Wrath
and play old Alberta Hunter songs.

the
good ones.

the
real ones.

it
went on
just like that...

day
after day,

until
the luck
finally ran out.

and
he was
good with that.

after the reading,

a
reporter
for the student paper

asked me
what career i would take

if
i wasn't a writer.

i
looked at him

and said:

at this point in my life
i guess
porn star
is out of the question.

the
poor kid
looked at me.

he
didn't
know what to say.

neither did i.

she

looked at
him and said:

"you're enough".

"enough for what?"

"for me."

with that,
she lay back

and
smiled.

they
never heard

the
rain.

she said:

of
course,
you know,
i AM your savior...

that thing we do,
over there

is
more
important
than god, or
church or prayer.

Christ,
you're
right (he said).

come here...

and
show me
what you mean.

she used to

feel
sorry for herself
in that way only the young can have.

at
bars
she'd
walk up
to a guy and
say *you've got*
hands like Michaelangelo's DAVID,

and
they'd
look at her
like she was crazy
and they wouldn't understand.

she'd have
6 tequilas straight off,

and dance
like there was no tomorrow.

it was
no surprise, then,
when she turned up dead

one sunday morning...

skirt torn, face
shot off,

blood

on the bathroom wall...

and
neither
Michaelangelo

nor
David

gave a holy good god damn.

the interviewer

didn't
know what
to make of it
when she asked me:

*in
case
of a fire,
what's the
first thing you would grab?*

and
i answered:

"my balls".

Charley

accused
her of being evil.

in
fact,
she did
get pleasure
out of watching

her
friends
destroy themselves.

Charley
would say
something like:

i
knew
things was good,

but,
they weren't,

and
he was right.

she was

just
like the others...

just
like the rest...

just
plain

evil.

i worked in a phone room once...

selling
light bulbs
over the phone.

can you
imagine that?

god-damn light bulbs.

it
was in
this little office
on the second floor

above
a pool room,

with
folding tables set up
with chairs and maybe 16 phones.

we each
had a stack of sheets
with names of prospects.

i
don't know
where they got the names

or
why,

because
it didn't matter.

because
no one ever bought the bulbs.

i
don't
even remember

how
we were
supposed to take an order

and
all i did
was dial the phone,

make
my pitch and
wait for them to hang up.

which they always did.

the job
lasted maybe
a couple of days
before i got tired of it

and
stopped going.

the
whole place

smelled of sweat

and
desperation

and
a certain
kind of failure
you never can forget.

this

is
a place

of
whispers.

the neighbor's dog

is
old

and
deaf.

she
sleeps all day,

pees
on the rug

and
throws up
every chance she gets.

i
promise
i won't do
that poet thing

and
compare
myself to her.

i
can't.

i'm
not deaf yet,

and
it's been weeks

since
i even
came close

to
peeing
on the rug.

he said:

reading
all
the
crap
poems
that
come
in
the mail

day after day, after day...

i
realize:

maybe
i really *do*

have
something

interesting

to
say

Peggy

had
a tooth
missing in front,
and when she talked,

it
made
a whistle.

Peggy Whistle was 43,
loved Scotch,
and

worked nights
at the D&J Diner.

she
also loved
her little dog, Blue.

Blue
came to
work with her
and slept on a ratty
old pillow in the back,

lifting
his head up
every time the door
opened and the bell above it rang.

Peggy never whistled any tunes,

although
you can't say
she didn't know any.

there
was that one
her father taught her...

you know the one...

about
that road to
wherever the hell it went.

names didn't matter much to Peg.

nothing
did, except

for Blue
and the sound of that bell,

and
a ring
that she wore

on
her hand
after work.

she
got it
from Tim,

or
Romeo,

or
Bill...

or
whatever
the hell was
the name of that dear,

sweet man.

Jesus, it

felt like
the kiss of death
when the professor wrote
and said she liked my poems
because they were amusing and irreverent

and i
wanted to
go out and shoot
myself in the back yard
just so i could break the chain

it's not
that she wasn't
a nice lady and was
paying me nicely to speak
at the school and i told her that
she should really take that money and

hire
three *real* poets instead,
as i was just a fake who got up
every morning, had my coffee, fed
the dog and came down here to fight with

the
words the
world the poems

and you.

when

it
came

to
him,

she
always

knew

that
much

was
never

more.

Tommy

lay
back
against
the rock,

and,
putting
his hands
behind his head

said

man,
i could use
me some more of

that
Joanie...

she
sure was
something,

wasn't she?

her
and that
red hair of hers.

he chose to

do
his suffering

in
grand style...

starting off
with beer in the morning,

then
the good wine
as the afternoon and
the memories kicked in.

toward evening

he
switched
to Grey Goose

and
finished the night
with his old friend, tequila.

it
wasn't much,
but it was all he had...

besides,

when
the checks came,

they

covered the rent,

and
the Goose and
every now and then,

even
the food.

the
poems
he wrote got
worse and worse...

eventually,
the mail stopped coming

and
there was
absolutely nothing

on t.v.

the final question

the interviewer asked was:
if you had to narrow it down
to just one thing,
what's the most important quality
for a writer to have?

by that time of the night
i was bored and more than a little bit tired

and i wanted
more than anything else
to get out of there
and go home,

but,
i figured i at least owed it to her
to play along with the game,
so i looked her in the eye
and said:

you really wanna know?
it's the ability
to ignore
the obvious.

it was getting late...
for me...
for the interview...
for everything.

i
didn't

have the time
to add that most of
the artists i look up to
(living and dead)
are the embodiment
of that old Tom Waits song...

the
one about
having a bad liver
and a broken heart.

i should
have also told her
that tenacity and courage

are a big part of it, too.

and...
yes...for sure...

the
ability
to ignore the obvious

and
look the other way.

Gwen said

her
name
meant
face of god,

or something like that.

i
don't know
where or how
she got that idea,

but she stuck with it,

right
to the end.

right up to
the time when she went

face to face

with a guy who swore
his name
meant:

he who devours
ham on rye.

she

had
the gift
of recreational shallowness...

she
knew
how to be

trivial...

and
how to avoid
emotional excess.

what
she didn't

know...

what
she couldn't

do...

was
figure
a way past Tommy.

he
may have
been creepy,

and
his smile

at times was

blank...

but,
that tat of his...

that
god damn tattoo...

sure
looked sweet.

she said

she
was pleased
to finally meet
a "genuine" author.

i
write
a little, myself,

she
said...

and
one day
i'm gonna
publish a book

that's
gonna knock
everyone's socks off.

including
yours.

she
looked sad

as
she
asked

exactly
what kind
of writer are you,

any way?

i
signed
the book...

handed
it to her, and

walking
away

mumbled:

*the
failed kind.*

the editor asked

for
a bunch
of my drinking poems.

old stuff.

he
didn't care
what they were
or where they were from

or
even
if they
had been
published before.

he
just
wanted
drinking poems.

odd,
since i haven't
had a decent drink

in
years...

not
since
the stroke
that got me
doing herbal tea

and fruit juice and water.

i've
even
learned
to like it.

kinda.

but
it's kept
me alive and
writing, so, i guess
there's no one to blame

for all this mess,

except

you

and the wine

and
me.

Acknowledgements

Some of these poems originally appeared in the following print and electronic books, magazines, and anthologies: Bayou Review, Beat The Dust, Boston Poetry, Carnival Lit, Chiron Review, Clock Radio, Cultural Weekly, Daily Dope Fiend, Degenerate Literature, Elephant, Epic Rites Journal, Epic Rites Review, Every Reason, Fekt, Fluorescent Stilts For Your Uncle, Gutter Eloquence, Heroin Love Songs, Indigent a la Carte, Into The Void, Kiss My Poetry, Lummox Journal, Mad Rush, Mas Tequila Review, Meat For Tea, Metropolis, Open Arts Forum, Orange Room Review, Outlaw Poetry, Penman Review, Pigeonbike, Preoccupied With Austin, Queen Mob, Ramingo's Porch, Rat Creek Press, Rogues Of The Red Baron Bar, Rufous, Sacramento Poetry, Short Story Library, St. Vitus, Street Poet Review, Superheroes, The Australian Times, The Exuberant Ashtray, The Smoking Typewriter, The Valley Review, Toledo Free Press, Tree Killer Ink, Unadorned Reader, Unokudo, Unrorean, Word Fountain, Zygote In My Coffee, 1/25, 12 Shotgun Blasts From The Underground

Also by John Yamrus

Five Dogs
Phoebe And Ito Are Dogs
RMA
Memory Lane
As Real As Rain
I Admit Nothing
Burn
Endure
Alchemy
Bark
They Never Told Me This Would Happen
Can't Stop Now!
Doing Cartwheels On Doomsday Afternoon
New And Selected Poems
Blue Collar
Shoot The Moon
One Step at a Time
78 RPM
Keep The Change
New And Used
Start To Finish
Someone Else's Dreams (novel)
Something
Poems
Those
Coming Home
American Night
15 Poems
Heartsongs
Lovely Youth (novel)
I Love

About the Author

In a career spanning more than 50 years as a working writer, **John Yamrus** has published 27 volumes of poetry, two novels, three volumes of non-fiction, and a children's book. He has also had more than 2,000 poems published in magazines and anthologies around the world.

Selections of his work have been translated into multiple foreign languages, including Spanish, Swedish, French, Japanese, Italian, Romanian, Albanian, Estonian, and Bengali. His poetry is taught in numerous colleges and universities.

He lives in Pennsylvania with his wife Kathy and dog Stella.

Visit John's website: http://www.johnyamrus.com

Made in the USA
Coppell, TX
02 February 2021